Theoethnimusicology:

VOLUME 1 – NOTHIN' BUT DA BLUES

Cedrick Von Jackson

Copyright © 2016 Cedrick Von Jackson

All rights reserved.

ISBN - 13: 978-0-692-64101-9

DEDICATION

For my wfie, Eulanda (Yogi)
The Music of My Heart.

CONTENTS

Acknowledgments	i
You Ain't Strong Enough For This Prayer	1
I've Been Thinking About Stories	4
Bobby Socks	6
Broken Mirrors	8
Warriors	11
The Violent Ones	13
Déjà vu	16
For Ms. Loretta Lynch	19
Haiku – Tally Marks	22
For The Homeless (Incomplete)	24
No White Flags	26
Haiku – Cycles	28
Haiku – Friendly Fire	30
Otis	32
Reruns	34
Somebody Prayed	36
Isaac	38
Sonnet – Ode To The Financial Divide	41
Too Young	43
We	45
Calvary	47

A Sonnet For Odessa	50
Sonnet – Photo Shoot	52
A Sonnet For Rahab	54
Haiku – For Charleston	56
For Charleston #2	58
Happy Birthday	60
Same Hurt, Different Day	63
Untitled	65
Haiku – Questions	68
Unplanned Pregnancy	70
Untitled – In Memory of Preachers and Pastors . . .	72
Untitled – A Prayer	75
My Blues Is	77
Brotherhood	80
Objective	82
About The Author	84
Coming Soon	85
Stormy Weather Suite	86
Stuff (The Edited Version)	87

PREFACE

"The blues was like that problem child that you may have had in the family. You was a little bit ashamed to let anybody see him, but you loved him. You just didn't know how other people would take it."

B.B. King

Honestly, I don't know how the reader will respond to the poems on these pages. Many of these pieces tell the "ugly." But sometimes we have to let our ugly show. That's what I feel the Blues does. It lets the ugly show, and then it dares to sing in spite of the ugly. Sometimes, I let my ugly show, and then I dare to write about it. Sometimes America let's her ugly show, and then we dare to sing about it, write about it, paint about it. That's the task of the artist; to be daring enough to expose the ugly. Give yourself permission to let your ugly show. Then dare to sing about it! It IS true what they say; "THE BLUES IS ALRIGHT!"

**In this volume of Theoethnimusicology, you will have the opportunity to journal along with each poem. If you are "feeling it," use the journal space to take the "Theoethnimusicology Challenge," writing your own poetry. Be courageous! Some of these poems follow a certain style. If you would like to write along these lines, a brief explanation of each style will be provided. There is a poet within you!

ACKNOWLEDGMENTS

First and foremost, I thank God for the gifts and talents with which I have been entrusted. To God be the glory, who doeth all things well.

I thank my beautiful wife, Eulanda Kaye Jackson, for her undying love and support, not only with this project, but with all of those crazy ideas and dreams that continue to pop into my head. I love you!

I thank my children, Jalise and Myles for their love and patience with me as I write and minister. Daddy loves you guys!

I thank my family, with whom I have learned to laugh, cry, and discuss "agenda items."

Special thanks goes out to the members of Mt. Zion Missionary Baptist Church of Sardis, MS. It has been through serving you that I have found a huge portion of my "voice."

"The Blues tell the story of life's difficulties, and if you think for a moment, you will realize that they take the hardest realities of life and put them into music, only to come out with some new hope or sense of triumph. This is triumphant music."

Martin Luther King, Jr.

YOU AIN'T STRONG ENOUGH FOR THIS PRAYER

You ain't strong enough for this prayer
Shoulders too un-broad to carry these burdens
This prayer's got deep roots
Like ancient trees
Nurtured by soil tilled by ancestors passed
And moaning moans too deep to understand
By anything other than Spirit

Your hands ain't held a garden hoe long enough
Too tender are your palms
Knees ain't been bent long enough
For you to understand this struggle
This prayer's got scars and wrinkles
From ages of scowling from pain
That birthed kings who were stolen away

Your young ears too tender to comprehend
The cries of those sold out to slavery
Of mothers separated from sons
Fathers separated from daughters
This prayer's filled with song mournfully sung
Over cotton plants under eyes of scrutiny
And behind closed creaking doors

This prayer's been passed down through story
Told round pot-bellied stoves
Shared by candlelight
Under hushed voice like secret
And your teeth ain't been cut long enough
Still feeding on milk
Like baby suckling at momma's breast

You ain't ready for this prayer
But one day you'll need it

CEDRICK VON JACKSON

Theoethnimusicology Challenge: Write a poem on the subject of prayer.

"The blues ain't nothing but a good man feelin' bad."

Leon Redbone

I'VE BEEN THINKING ABOUT STORIES

I've been thinking about stories lately
How important is their telling
How we used to have such a strong oral tradition
Where those stories were told
While scratching dandruff
Sitting around pot-bellied stoves
Sitting around dinner tables
Sitting around campfires
Under bush arbors
On brownstone stoops

I've been thinking about what those stories taught
How they encouraged
How they reminded
How they guided and guarded
How they healed us

I've been thinking about stories lately
Tell me my mother's stories
Give me grandmother's and grandfather's wisdom
Let me know where I came from
So I know where I go from here

Tell me the story of how my blood came to be
What courses it ran through to course through my veins

I want to know the story of the trees
Know why the mimosa tree goes to sleep at night
And why the cypress tree bends knees
In the muddy swamp

And the drum beats
And our dance
Stories told on grandpa's knee
Sitting in the swing under the old persimmon tree
Ancient to new stories
That come full circle

Tell me
I am waiting

Theoethnimusicology Challenge: Write a poem about your favorite childhood story/memory.

BOBBY SOCKS

Little girl walking
Bobby socks lace pristine white
Hair in pig tails short cute
Carrying armful of books
Because you desire more
Than the monsters
Creeping behind kudzu
Down dusty southern roads
They are afraid of you
You know
Afraid of your smart
Terrified by your pretty
Intimidated by fire in eyes
Fire in soul
Fire in heart
Fire in mouth
Tell them truth
They will tremble
Story them into submission
They will be amazed
Bobby socks pristine white
Should not walk
Not like you
Bobby socks pristine white
Should have dust on them
Especially down these roads
But your mama warned you
Way before you left home
Keep your socks clean
And keep walking

Theoethnimusicology Challenge: Write a poem about a time you had to "keep walking" in the face of adversity.

CEDRICK VON JACKSON

BROKEN MIRRORS

She stares
In the mirror
And quickly she can hear the sound
Of last night's argument
And how it all went down
In a drunken rage that brother swung on her
She said one word to him and then he sprung on her
Bloody nose bloody eyes
Bloody tear drops
Bloody lips bloody blouse
Bloody high tops
And all that she could do was just fall back
He left a message on the phone waiting for call backs
But this ain't no audition
There ain't no casting couch
She ain't no Covergirl but
She covers up the ouch
How could she just call him back after all that he had done
And to make them matters worse it was done before her son
Now what about his future
How could he understand
Could he learn to break the cycle
Would he be a better man
She went down to the church in search of love affection
Holy-roller church folk pointed in the wrong direction
Constantly quoting scripture to help fix her plight
Joy comes in the morning weeping only endures for a night
Well that's all well and good but where's the real help
She's at the end of her rope
She cannot help herself
She tries to call her mother
She tries to phone a friend
She's looking for a lifeline
To help this nightmare end
She cries herself to sleep pillow wet with tears
What did she ever do to deserve to live in constant fear

Day 2 same song different verse
Still looking for some aid to help her break this vicious curse
She starts to wonder when and where was God
His presence seemed pretty ABSENT now that was odd

Should she pack her bags and leave to make a better life
Has this brother left her bitter she been scarred for life
Could be could be not I don't know who's to say
Looking in the mirror thinking gotta be a better way
Gotta be a better life
Gotta be some sunshine
Ray-ban lifestyle putting all the gray behind
Negative in her past positive in her future
Never putting up with all the evil things that she use to
Looking out for her son
Yeah he's the only one
Old life left behind her
New life just begun
Cause she found that real Christ
Who can wipe those tears from eyes
God has promised that He'll love her better than she realized
The One who'll never beat her
He took those stripes for her
She was at the point of death
He gave His life for her

The person that she sees in the mirror looking back
Smiling big Standing tall
Heart full Love in tact
No more Covergirl covering up black eyes
Finally found a true love to her surprise
No more Covergirl covering up black eyes
Finally found a true love to her surprise

Theoethnimusicology Challenge: Write a poem in honor and support of someone you know is suffering relationship abuse.

WARRIORS

Listen
Let me tell tales
Stories of strong soldiers
Who will not be afraid of fight
Or strife

Theoethnimusicology Challenge: Write a short poem about victories you would like to hear tale of.

THE VIOLENT ONES

Matthew 11:12 - And from the days of John the Baptist until now the kingdom of heaven suffers violence, and the violent take it by force.

We are the ones
Rushing into the streets
With fists and signs held high
Arms linked like chained fence
Daring to lift song
Audacious enough to expect
Good news
We don't have to burn down
To prove we have fire
It's been burning in us
Since before ancestors discovered it
We are powder keg
Waiting to explode
If one more falls
We wouldn't trade nothing
For our journey now
We are Crips and Bloods
Disciples and Lords
Calling momentary truce
For what is done against us
Is greater than what we
Do to each other
We are beyond
Beating swords into plowshares
We still study war
But with a new war plan
War games are over
Baltimore is the new Galilee
Ferguson the new Judea
And we march for
No more broken backs
And shot in backs
No more choke holds
And found in back seats
Hands cuffed behind
But dead by self-inflicted
Gun shot wounds

No more twelve-year olds
Shot in about one and a half seconds
We flood the streets
Looking for Gospel
Longing for Good News
No more will be our Good News
No more will be our Good News

Theoethnimusicology Challenge: Write a poem about standing up for justice.

CEDRICK VON JACKSON

DEJA VU

It was like
Two shots in the dark
Body laying cold in the park
Now life is looking grim and stark
And no herald angels singing hark

The spark of life was snuffed out
Music tuned out by a mother's cries and shouts
And we still talking bout how black lives mattered
While every day more blood is splattered
On concrete sidewalks

And we pray Thy kingdom come Thy will be done
All the while wondering if we'll see the rising Son
Begun or begin with original sin
Then Cain killed Abel got the first murder rap
Every since then we've been falling in the trap

Brother against brother, sister on mother
Riot, loot, steal from one another
We can't breathe cuz the tear gas smothers
Trayvon, Tamir Rice, Mike Brown and many others

Found no justice in the land of the free
Committing gross crimes against all humanity
My country tis of thee from sea to shining sea
Hands stretched out like Lady Liberty

Bring me your tired, your poor, your huddled masses
So I can divide them up into low and middle classes
And nobody learns, we all got hall passes
And the movement starts with the roots and the grasses
That's grassroots

Wall Street getting heavy doses of the air up there
Your Street getting by on a wing and a prayer
Your Street talking bout life ain't fair
Wall Street steadily climbing the golden stair
Where did we go wrong

We protest, we march, Selma déjà vu

Young folks fighting over J's hardly got a clue
Grown folks talking bout what we gone do
And we all fail the test of two answers – false or true
It's true

Now we all grasping for answers
Like pulling straws
Sad thing is we keep getting the short end of the stick
And instead of heirs getting rich the air is getting thick
And we still can't breathe
Sad thing is we keep getting the short end of the stick
And instead of heirs getting rich the air is getting thick
And we still can't breathe

Theoethnimusicology Challenge: Write a poem dedicated to any "movement" you believe in.

FOR MS. LORETTA LYNCH

It is ironic isn't it
For a vote to be held so long
For a woman of your stature
With a name like yours

Lynch
Say it means
Hang
Murder
Assassinate
Mob
Kill
But your vote came
And you rose above a name
Above a nation

Only wanting to make a difference
Instead you made history
Another in a long line of firsts
How does first feel
Does it cause head held high
Chest stuck out
Smile on face
Do you feel like a winner
Like a victor
Or has the fight
Just now begun

And what are we still fighting for
Equality
Justice
Rights
Love
Peace
And what sense does
Fighting for peace make

But thank you
For fighting
Standing
Waiting

Praying
Thank you
Ms. Lynch

Theoethnimusicology Challenge: Write a poem dedicated to a strong woman in your life, past or present.

HAIKU – TALLY MARKS

Writing on walls
Counting down lives and years
TOO MUCH TO NUMBER

Theoethnimusicology Challenge: Write a haiku – a three-lined poem that has five syllables in the first line, seven syllables in the second line, and five syllables in the third line – about counting down to some greatly anticipated event.

CEDRICK VON JACKSON

FOR THE HOMELESS (INCOMPLETE)

And the snow kept falling all around
While all on the ground they slept
We stepped over them
Never lending our shoulder to them

And their home is cardboard boxes
Filled with dirty socks its
A shame low down dirty rotten
How much we've forgotten that
It could be us instead of them
And yet we're the ones singing hymns
To a God who knows our plight
And lights our night
Our battles He will fight
While they keep fighting for their lives

Can you spare a dollar makes me wanna holler
Except it's not my hands that get thrown up
And it's not my hands that get held out to reach them
And every time one dies qualifies my hands to bleach them
Lifeblood of the innocent on guilty hands
Because I never truly did what Christ demands
I played the spectator sitting in the stands
Of this game called life while
Where their next meal comes from is their daily strife
It's gotta be brutal out there on those streets
Where no weapon formed against ends in defeat
And I'll never leave you nor forsake you
Turns into whatever don't kill you breaks you
And while you're deciding it's the Jordans that makes you
Not one bit of knowledge of their struggle breaks through
Your brain

Theoethnimusicology Challenge: Write a poem dedicated to the homeless situation in America.

NO WHITE FLAGS

Laying down ain't easy
On beds of concrete and nails
Sleepless are the nights
With thorn in side

Looking out windows
Proves difficult at best
When the future proves dim
And the sun won't rise

Makes me wonder
Do you remember the moment
When you first knew you were loved
How did it feel

Did it make concrete nail beds bearable
Could you rest easy with thorn in side
Do you remember the
Holding hands praying feeling

When you found out they had faith in you
Did your heart skip a beat
Even when the sun didn't shine
Or did it even matter

There will be no white flags tonight
No surrender
No throw in the towel
You have come too far to turn back

Horses led to water will drink
I will make it happen
If is it the last thing I do
This is promise

Theoethnimusicology Challenge: Write a poem about a time you had to persevere.

HAIKU - CYCLES

Funny how old folks
Become once again like babes
As death approaches

Theoethnimusicology Challenge: Write a haiku – a three-lined poem that has five syllables in the first line, seven syllables in the second line, and five syllables in the third line – about events that come in cycles.

HAIKU – FRIENDLY FIRE

Why are we fighting
Don't we know we are same team
Striving to get there

Theoethnimusicology Challenge: Write a haiku – a three-lined poem that has five syllables in the first line, seven syllables in the second line, and five syllables in the third line – about being on the same team.

OTIS

Your name means wealth
But in deep dark Mississippi woods
All your wealth was stolen from you
As you hung from tree

Were you followed home from the casino
After a lucky night
Of Blackjack or Mississippi Stud
Luck ran out it seems

Who did this and why
How could they
Did you do it to yourself
It is 2015 and we shudder to think

Is this same story different day
Are you the latest crop of strange fruit
Did mockingbirds sing at your demise
Did cypress tree bend knees to pray

Will they care enough for full investigation
Do you matter that much
Or will they assume you were just
One more casualty of self hate

And your death makes me wonder
If ever do we commit self hangings
In forests of solitude and silence
Because someone said, "Go kill yourself"

Theoethnimusicology Challenge: Write a poem depicting something (innocence, life, esteem, virginity, etc.) being stolen from someone.

RERUNS

Nothing but reruns
On the tube tonight
Every time I change the channel
There are tales of another plight

Another murder
More violence
Same old song
Another shooting
Another life gone wrong

CNN coverage
News anchors report
MSNBC and Fox
Tear down not exhort
Extort our lives of value
Hands up don't shoot
Protestors keep a marching
Riot burn and loot

But change the station and you will see
Scenes that look the same
Except instead of protest riots
They lament loss of games
And somehow that's ok

Even music channels play
Same ole tune
Same ole muddy water blues
Life snuffed out too soon

Time to find better programming
Time to make a change
Where peace and harmony and unity
Are common place and never strange
New times call for new signals
Like going digital from analog
That change was years ago
And we still tread the fog

Theoethnimusicology Challenge: Write a poem about news that you are tired of hearing about, but seems to be constantly broadcasted.

CEDRICK VON JACKSON

SOMEBODY PRAYED

Somebody prayed
For me
Called my name
Out loud
Down on knees
Worn rugged and calloused
By countless prayers
With words too deep
Too deep to mention
Words welling up
From secret places
Flanked by jasper and amethyst
Twelve gates to that city
Or so they say
This place of prayer
And hope and faith
Keep praying

Theoethnimusicology Challenge: Write a poem on the subject of prayer.

ISAAC

I suppose when your name means laughter
You should always get the joke
But I see nothing funny about knife raised overhead
The last image of an offering strapped to the altar of sacrifice

I see nothing funny about mother left out of the loop
Left home to do these "motherly things"
Whatever that means
While the caravan marches away falsely confident
That they shall all return safely
How do you know

I see nothing funny about Father marching to his high place of worship
Chanting and singing himself into a heightened stupor
While son is forced to carry the instruments of his own demise
We witness these horrors everyday
Do we not

I see nothing funny about these sacrifices
In the name of
In the name of
In the name of
I cannot say
Is this really what we do with our promise

I see nothing funny about the silence in your saunter
Do you not know that I wonder where is the lamb
Long before I ask the question
Say something

I see nothing funny about a son so trusting as to follow blindly
Asking only one question
Where is the "Dad, where are we going?"
Is there no, "Are we there yet?"
When was, "How much further is it" asked?

How do you know God will provide this time
Have you seen God provide like this before
What makes you so confident
Are you absolutely certain that it was God that you heard
And why are you so quick to start marching

When you hear random voices

Each step closer to summit of mountain
May as well be another step closer to edge of cliff
We march in silence
Slow steady silence
Will no one stop this death march
Will there be no call to halt

I know that I am supposed to be trusting
But this
Well what about you giving me
Something or someone to trust

Why is it so easy to sacrifice
What you have waited so long for
That you have prayed so hard for

I am miracle
Life born from dead womb
Now following dead beat dad
And I can tell that my questions make you nervous
From the tremble in your laugh
But I see nothing funny

CEDRICK VON JACKSON

Theoethnimusicology Challenge: Write a poem dedicated to a character in the Bible or other literary work who experienced struggle in their life.

SONNET – ODE TO THE FINANCIAL DIVIDE

If justice rolls down like a mighty stream
And hope lives on in dreams everlasting
What happens to pride that has lost it's steam
Regardless tears, prayer and fasting

Does joy lose it's way on life's beaten path
And peace give it's way to bullet and gun
And what of the laws of fury and wrath
That snuff out a life before it's begun

But what does God want 'cept justice and good
To protect the weak and infirmed and poor
What price must be waged for shelter and food
While rich men stay rich, we know this for sure

No man is an isle nor boat set adrift
Yet rich men and poor stare 'cross this wide rift

CEDRICK VON JACKSON

Theoethnimusicology Challenge: Write a sonnet – a fourteen-lined poem that has ten syllables in each line and follows an ABAB, CDCD, EFEF, GG rhyme pattern – about some area of injustice.

TOO YOUNG

Dearest little child
You are ten years old
What business do you have
Knowing about things
Like peeing in a cup
So your dad can
Use you to pass his drug test
These are not the tests
You should be worried about
Concern yourself with
Fractions and multiplication
The science of
Tornadoes in a bottle
And condensation and rain
You are ten years old

CEDRICK VON JACKSON

Theoethnimusicology Challenge: Write a poem dedicated to children who experience way too much at such a young age.

WE

We are the ones whose songs
Reverberate from the soil of cotton fields
We keep the chain gang's cadence
Steadily keeping the work

We built cities on the sweat of our brow
And received learning
From books out of date
And from teachers of the underclassed

We have trod roads of stone
Surviving branding rods
Fire hoses and attack dogs
Yet marching on undeterred

We have born burdens in heat of day
And walked through shadows of death
Undeterred and unfettered
Unbroken and pressing on

We are still trying to find
Crystal stairs to climb
Knowing wood will do
Rickety and broken yet going higher

We are still slain in the streets
But believe freedom is coming soon
So educate ourselves we must
Of a history woven in the tapestry of being

We are evolving and becoming
Greater than we have ever known
We once built great cities
We will again

With the Lord on our side

CEDRICK VON JACKSON

Theoethnimusicology Challenge: Write a poem dedicated to groups of people who have faced oppression.

CALVARY

Hills were not made for this
Hills were made to be alive
With sounds of music
Not cries of anguish
But Calvary, you were different

You were not just another
Mountain to climb
Not just another
Entry into record books
Calvary, you were different

You were skull and blood
Sweat and tears and anguish
You were beatings and hangings
Thorns, purple robes, and two thieves
Calvary, you were different

You were sun refused to shine
And curtain rent in two
You were dead men walking from graves
And earthquake; whole lot of shaking
Calvary, you were different

You were Father forgive them
It is finished and I thirst
Mother behold your son; son behold
Into thy hands; Eli lama sabathani; today paradise
Calvary, you were different

Surely you buttressed the Son of God
A lamb slain; a lion tamed; if only for a moment
A king unacknowledged by His own people
A Rose and Lily cut down too soon
Calvary, you were different

Though dark the night
You held bright and morning star
Amid constellation of three like Orion's belt
And thought it not robbery to let Him shine in darkest hour

Calvary, you were different

Many mounts strive to be you
Everest is not high enough
Kilimanjaro not nearly majestic as you
Fiji cannot comprehend your greatness
So, why even try

Theoethnimusicology Challenge: Write a poem dedicated to Jesus Christ and His work on Calvary or to a particular martyr of your choosing.

CEDRICK VON JACKSON

A SONNET FOR ODESSA

My grandmother's hands would knead biscuit dough
Then turn around and chop in the garden
Hard work and sweat made the vegetables grow
Up from soil that by sun had been hardened

At night before turning in we said prayers
Of the now I lay me down to sleep kind
Then tuck us away, give comfort to cares
We slept easy, no worries on our mind

Long days were spent on a fisherman's bank
No fancy casting rod, just a cane pole
Watching still waters, the bobbers they sank
While stories were told that nourished our soul

Back at the house we'd sweep dirt from the yard
Livin' easy, never knew had it hard

THEOETHNIMUSICOLOGY VOL. 1 – NOTHIN' BUT DA BLUES

Theoethnimusicology Challenge: Write a sonnet – a fourteen-lined poem that has ten syllables in each line and follows an ABAB, CDCD, EFEF, GG rhyme pattern – dedicated to your grandmother.

SONNET – PHOTO SHOOT

You have always brick housed and Barbie dolled
And thirty-six, Twenty-four, Thirty-sixed
Yourself into images reinstalled
By gazes of men whose eyesight was fixed

Do you know who you are underneath there
Or have you been duped by this gross system
Everyone knowing blues eyes and blonde hair
Only worn because you felt the victim

Know that your genetic make-up is pure
Since it came from the One who is Holy
Created in a great image for sure
Learn to appreciate yourself wholly

For this set we need not fake covergirls
But those who've been deemed ready for the world

Theoethnimusicology Challenge: Write a sonnet – a fourteen-lined poem that has ten syllables in each line and follows an ABAB, CDCD, EFEF, GG rhyme pattern – encouraging some young woman that she is "enough".

CEDRICK VON JACKSON

A SONNET FOR RAHAB

Can Rahab find unconditional love
She is the consummate business woman
So emotion's put away like old glove
Cuz customers, she must keep 'em comin'

For them she is all things, but none of self
She cannot afford cloudiness of mind
Get inside their heads to ensure her wealth
But her feelings she must keep in a bind

She needs roof over head, has mouths to feed
This alone is her primary focus
Because a mere shell from doing the deed
Pulling emotional hocus pocus

Painted on pretty face, cheeks red, smile fake
Never falls in love too much is at stake

Theoethnimusicology Challenge: Write a sonnet – a fourteen-lined poem that has ten syllables in each line and follows an ABAB, CDCD, EFEF, GG rhyme pattern – about a woman who does her best to make ends meet.

CEDRICK VON JACKSON

HAIKU – FOR CHARLESTON #1

Hands raised in the church
No more symbolize worship
But please don't shoot us

THEOETHNIMUSICOLOGY VOL. 1 – NOTHIN' BUT DA BLUES

Theoethnimusicology Challenge: Write a haiku – a three-lined poem that has five syllables in the first line, seven syllables in the second line, and five syllables in the third line – dedicated to rising above tragedy.

FOR CHARLESTON #2

We stand under the shadow of a cross
Unholy and fought for
Stars that lead to false navigation
Star spangled banner
Holding on to memories of oppression
Red for the blood of our ancestors
Shed in fields of cotton
And on auction blocks
Where field of dreams turned nightmare
Time and time again
Another man's aggression led to secession
A separation that was less than civil
So we warred
We fought
And continue to fight on
Brother against brother
Wolves in sheep's clothes
Unable to trust
The very ones who came to pray with us
Constant reminder of the struggle
A symbol refusing to bow
To the memory of our slain

Theoethnimusicology Challenge: Write a poem speaking against those things which seek to divide us.

CEDRICK VON JACKSON

HAPPY BIRTHDAY

December 15, 2014
Is a day I was glad to see
Let me tell you what I mean
You see, at the tender age of twelve
Tamir Rice was shot dead
And on the cold concrete
Another young soldier bled
Another mother cried
Another life was lost
Bodies stacking up paying terrible cost
And my son just made it
To a whole nother year
But as long as they packing guns
We still living in fear
No background checks
And when they check and fault is found
They still get jobs regardless of background
Mentally unfit still carrying a gun
Snuffing out lives before they've hardly begun
And we wait
Wait for another life to be lost
Bodies stacking up paying terrible cost
And my son just made it
To a whole nother year
But as long as they packing guns
We still living in fear
When I tell you this truth I must be realistic
Living past the age of twelve
Is the newest statistic
Death before heartbreak
Grave before girlfriend
Martyr before the masses
Endless cycle never end
Unfairly profiled because they fit the mold
Of the ones on the block where the drugs are sold
Rise against saggin' pants
Respectability politics
And we lose every battle
Fighting with rocks and sticks
And what they looting for
Don't they know it's their own community

Massive media coverage
Promoting massive disunity
Immunity is for the privileged
A luxury most ain't got
Protests around the world
While the block's still hot
And my son made thirteen
A whole nother year
He made it past twelve
But I'm still living in fear

Theoethnimusicology Challenge: Write a poem dedicated to your child(ren).

SAME HURT, DIFFERENT DAY

We facing hung juries
Passing non-indictments
People walk in darkness
Searching for enlightenment
Justice being carried out
In kangaroo courts
Judicial system in critical condition
Only living with help from life support
Truth lying dead in streets
Righteousness standing back, hands folded
Privilege takes grand stand
Unfair verdict already molded
AK's in some hands
Nerf guns in others
Wal-Mart hands up
Senseless cries of mothers
#blacklivesmatter
#handsupdontshoot
#icantbreathe
Some cry peace, others cry loot
Strange fruit used to hang from trees
Now it's harvested in streets
They say we're making progress
But I'm witnessing years retreat
Twelve years old never made it to temple
Had no chance for Father's business
When power lies in hands of some
There's always conflicting witness
Four against one
Officer never broke hold
Got it all on tape
Autopsy reports death by lethal chokehold
Non-indicted getting paid
Victim's family disregarded
Left to lament to grieve to mourn
Memories of their dear departed
Non-indicted getting paid
Victim's family disregarded
Left to lament to grieve to mourn
Memories of their dear departed

CEDRICK VON JACKSON

Theoethnimusicology Challenge: Write a poem depicting pain that occurs over and over again.

UNTITLED

Slavery
Bravery of a people
Fighting for their rights
Just to be treated equal
Big dipper catching tears of the mothers
Gun shots ring out taking out the brothers
Friendly fire
How much more blood will we require
Casting shade
Jealous of each other's stand of lemonade
Rest in peace MLK and we're still dreaming
But we're still marching in the streets still screaming
Really I understand the depth of your frustration
Phenomenon spreading all across the nation
But the question is why we still fighting
When there are all these wrongs needing righting
Lack of education
Lack of health care
Senseless segregation
Looking for the first rung of the crystal stair
Langston Hughes
B.B. King got us singing better blues
Mo' better

Poverty
Living from pay check to pay check
Living at break neck pace
Understanding that the race
Is not given to the swift
But to the holy livin'
How come we can't get no breaks
Hard to tell the difference
Between the real and the fakes
We're not clowns but we're still
Tracing tracks of our tears
Been begging for years
For bread at tables of plenty
I'd take the crumbs
That fall from the master's table
Call me a dog if you want to
I can take it

CEDRICK VON JACKSON

Just as long as my family has enough
Food so we can make it
Welfare commodity
Cheddar only goes so far
When the rent's due

Theoethnimusicology Challenge: What gives you the blues? Write a poem dedicated to your own personal blues.

CEDRICK VON JACKSON

HAIKU - QUESTIONS

What if I told you
Tomorrow was a vapor
Always taunting souls

Theoethnimusicology Challenge: Write a haiku – a three-lined poem that has five syllables in the first line, seven syllables in the second line, and five syllables in the third line – about a question you have yet to be answered.

CEDRICK VON JACKSON

UNPLANNED PREGNANCY

You were pregnant
With hope of justice
But swallowed whole
The pill of abortion
And the tears of our loss
Is being gassed out of us

You miscarried
And felt no sadness
This was the baby
Unwanted in the first place
And the blood on your hand
Never mattered to you

Theoethnimusicology Challenge: Using "pregnancy," "abort" or "miscarry" as a metaphor, write a poem about a time you felt like giving up on a dream.

UNTITLED – IN MEMORY OF PREACHERS/PASTORS WHO CONTEMPLATE OR CARRY OUT SUICIDE

I would not dare ask
That you walk a mile in my shoes
This journey you would not understand
It has been more painful
Than you could ever know
And I love you too much
To see you go through
What I know I must

Even when you walk with me
I walk alone
Subconsciously holding in
Those things you would use against me
If you knew the whole story

You have pedestaled me
Unaware that I am afraid of heights
You have spotlighted me
Unknowingly
I get stage fright
My hand trembles
Trembles
Trembles

I hold my tears in one hand
Your prayers in the other
And they all slip through my fingertips
Tears and prayers
Like life giving water
Wasted on parched desert

I am not allowed to
Throw in the towel
Wave the white flag
I must show faith
Because your faith needs reassurance

I am character and caricature

Actor on stage playing the part
For your applause
Step and fetch it
Because part of me needs reassurance
And you can never know

You will never know about
The attempt to take my life
Unless I succeed

You will say this makes me
Somehow less holy
But I was human
Before I was holy

CEDRICK VON JACKSON

Theoethnimusicology Challenge: Write a poem dedicated to someone who attempted suicide.

UNTITLED – A PRAYER

This prayer
This sigh
This moan and groan
This pain through which we rock
This sway back and forth
To song we know but cannot sing
Cannot hum
Cannot tune
Only rock and sway
And this stare into no where
Seeing both nothing and everything
And embrace, this embrace
One slips through hands
But never from heart
Never forget
We would if we could
Then would not dare
And this cry
Ohhhh this cry
This sorrow
This pain
This why now God
This why me Lord
This gone too soon
This gone way too soon

CEDRICK VON JACKSON

Theoethnimusicology Challenge: Write a poem dedicated to prayer.

MY BLUES IS

Come here chil'
Let me teach you
How to Blues

Let me teach you
Song in strange land
Wanna hang up yo harps
And weep like willows
By rivers of sorrow
Tears drownin' in the current

Let me teach you
Down on your knees
Prayin' till
Sweat runs like blood
While others sleep

Learn these lessons
On overturned washtubs
By pot-bellied stoves
Hummin' tunes
Of our emancipation

You see my Blues ain't always sad
They don't always cry
They lament and laugh
They are weepin' endurin'
And joy comin' in mornin'

My Blues ain't always sad
They are Rough side of mountain
And smoothin' up the rough way
They are fight on ole soldier
And study war no mo'

My Blues ain't always sad
They come in shades of
How I got over and
Trouble don't last always
So I keep on sangin'

CEDRICK VON JACKSON

I have had the Blues
Forced out of me
By sangin' good ole work songs
Keepin' cadence so I could
Keep up wit' the work
And you can't sang my Blues
Less you know where I been
Been through what I've known
Trod stony roads
In heat of weary years

You can't sang my Blues
Less you had yo' heart broke
In a million pieces
And had to glue them together
With the paste of your own tears

My mournful melodies
Have been sung by mothers
Of sons gunned down in streets
And wayward souls longin'
For refuge in pilgrim lands

My Blues are lullabies
For homeless soldiers
Who shelter down
In cardboard boxes while
Wall Street Execs stroll by

The beauty in my Blues
Ain't in notes correctly sung
But in the hope that
With all I am given
I have the nerve to sing

I have the nerve to sing

THEOETHNIMUSICOLOGY VOL. 1 – NOTHIN' BUT DA BLUES

Theoethnimusicology Challenge: Write a poem dedicated to your own personal blues.

CEDRICK VON JACKSON

BROTHERHOOD

We are brothers
Birthed from wombs of strength
Nurtured by the sun of a million years
We know each other's struggle
I am your keeper
I will not Cain and Abel you
But will enable you
Your blood will not flow through the street
And cry out from broken pavement
I will empower you
To reach higher
Past forbidden fruit
You will grasp stars
Shouldering the world
Is not too much to ask
If we prop each other up
Your cross I will help bear
We will face Gethsemane together
You will not be slept on
I will stand and keep watch
What we build will soar
Better, farther, higher
Than Wilbur and Orville's created wings
We will ascend like eagles
We are more than a handshake
We are heart and soul
Dapped up in brotherly love
Inseparable
One unified
Brotherhood

Theoethnimusicology Challenge: Write a poem dedicated to true brotherhood or sisterhood.

OBJECTIVE

If the objective is to be effective
It must encompass the entire collective
And what we find in being retrospective
Is that often time our objective is too selective

All it takes is a reflective look
To understand that the footsteps our ancestors took
May not be written in the history book
And so our narrative demands a closer look

Look what was built with the loads on their back
While facing Jim Crow and vicious attack
It was resources, not wisdom, they'd often lack
But somehow someway they kept their lives on track

Help me remember that our redemption story
Is more than a wishful allegory
Filled with hope, not depleted of glory
Not destined to become a sideshow on Maury

Povich which many of us find entertaining
Shucking and jiving, living life by no-braining
And if we keep up the foolishness, not much will be remaining
But many of us would rather just sit back complaining

About the man and the system not seeming to care
Well my name ain't Langston, I build my own crystal stair
My objective, keep climbing stormy weather or fair
And I hope your objective is to meet me there

Theoethnimusicology Challenge: Choose and "AMAZING" word, and write a poem with your amazing word as its title.

ABOUT THE AUTHOR

Born in Memphis, TN and raised in Coldwater, MS, Cedrick Von Jackson acknowledges that his path has been guided by God and Spirit and shaped through the arts. As an ordained minister and Baptist pastor, he has published sermons and sermon illustrations in "The African American Pulpit" and at www.theafricanamericanlectionary.org. As an actor on the community theatre stage, he has performed in musicals like "The Music Man," "The Fantasticks," "A Chorus Line," and a special performance of "The Wiz" with Memphis Black Repertory Theatre and the Memphis Symphony Orchestra, as well as Neil Simon's "Proposals," and the hit "Driving Miss Daisy." As a poet, he has published a previous work entitled *"Following the Breadcrumb Path: Navigating the Journey Toward God, Justice, and Love."* Cedrick has been writing poetry for over ten years, and can be found blogging at www.literallyced.wordpress.com.

COMING SOON

Theoethnimusicology
Vol. 2
"We Cool Like Dat"

(excerpts)

CEDRICK VON JACKSON

Stormy Weather Suite

Rainy day music
Sounds just as sweet as sunshine
On a hot tin roof

Stormy weather songs
Chase all the sorrows away
And leave me joyful

Sweet raindrop rhythms
Staccato off the sidewalk
Dictate my dancing

Stuff (The Edited Version)

I've got stuff in me
Yeah that's a good word for it
Stuff
Stuff like
Hopefulness over disappointment
Hatred and dissent
I'm too afraid to admit out loud
And it keeps coming out
In dreams that won't let me sleep
In my dreams
Folks who've hurt me
Get a double portion of stuff
Because in my dreams
I'm a baddddddd man
Fully in control of my stuff
Walk softly and carry a big stick
So I can beat the stuff out of this stuff
I would call them rainbows
But my tongue won't allow me to do that
They are colorful though, these rainbows
But they only paint in terms of casting shade
Oak trees
You see rainbows are not supposed to bring color
They're supposed to bring promise
So these rainbows ain't doing their job
I just wish a rainbow would do its job
And help me find a pot of gold
And if it weren't for leprechauns
Life would be so much easier
Magical even
But leprechauns in my dreams
Only hide stuff

Yeah that's a good word for it
STUFF

www.ingramcontent.com/pod-product-compliance
Lightning Source LLC
Chambersburg PA
CBHW060209050426
42446CB00013B/3028